STAR WARS MEMORABILIA

An Unofficial Guide to *Star Wars* Collectables

Paul Berry

AMBERLEY

Acknowledgements

The author would like to thank the following for their help with this book: Vectis Toy Auctions, Andy Davies, Tony Ratten, Paul Riches, Adam Berryman, Chris Jacklin, Jason Freeman, Roger Dobson and Mighty Jabba Collection.

First published 2018

Amberley Publishing
The Hill, Stroud
Gloucestershire, GL5 4EP

www.amberley-books.com

Copyright © Paul Berry, 2018

The right of Paul Berry to be identified as the Author of this work has been asserted in accordance with the Copyrights, Designs and Patents Act 1988.

ISBN 978 1 4456 7644 9 (print)
ISBN 978 1 4456 7645 6 (ebook)

British Library Cataloguing in Publication Data.
A catalogue record for this book is available from the British Library.

Typesetting by Amberley Publishing.
Printed in the UK.

Contents

Introduction

A little over forty years ago, a new science fiction film appeared in cinemas. While we now think of *Star Wars* as a huge sprawling saga, back in 1977 the name '*Star Wars*' referred to only one movie and no one could have had any idea that the films and their merchandising would become so vast and endure for so long.

While at an early stage George Lucas had merchandising in the back of his mind, licensing *Star Wars* proved a tough sell initially. Many of the major toy companies shied away from the film and a novelisation and comic adaptation were the only major items to arrive ahead of the movie.

After being turned down by some of the major toy companies, Kenner, a subsidiary of the General Mills corporation, were awarded the toy license. Kenner's small 3¾ action figures are now one of the products most associated with *Star Wars* and one of the most collectable, but there were hundreds of other items of merchandising available from various manufacturers. Never had tie-in merchandise been available on such a scale before. *Star Wars* soon set a trend where toy lines and associated products became a prerequisite for many blockbuster movies. It reshaped toy aisles and popularised the concept of the action

figure. Companies desperate for a slice of *Star Wars*' success launched similar lines, many based around other film and television properties such as *Star Trek* and *The Black Hole*.

For a child growing up in the 1980s, Star Wars was the biggest thing there was. But in some way the collectables meant more than the films, precisely because it wasn't that easy to see the movies outside of their runs at the cinema. It is hard to put over to anyone who wasn't there at the time how exciting a visit to the local toy shop was and how great the Star Wars toy displays usually were. In a time before the internet, there was no telling when new items would be available, and finding a figure you had never seen before was one of the most exciting things to a ten-year-old.

But then one day Star Wars just went away. Following the release of *Return of the Jedi* in 1983, interest in *Star Wars* had gradually begun to wane. George Lucas had tentative plans to make films telling the early adventures of Obi Wan Kenobi and Anakin Skywalker, but there was no timescale given for such films and some came to doubt they would ever be made.

The late eighties are now regarded as a wilderness period and it wasn't until the nineties that *Star Wars* gradually returned to the public's consciousness, and since then has never really gone away.

New *Star Wars* media such as the prequel films, the animated series and now the new era of films from Walt Disney have constantly attracted new fans. *Star Wars* is being experienced by a third generation of *Star Wars* fans; the children of the 1980s are now middle-aged and those who grew up on the prequels are in their mid-twenties and early thirties. It seems distinctly possible that *Star Wars* and its associated products will continue to endure throughout the years, possibly outliving all of us who collect today.

Collecting *Star Wars* can be a daunting experience and the volume of product is now so vast that it can be hard to know where to start. Having a focus is a good starting point, whether it be action figures or comics or even products based on particular characters. Collecting everything is a dream few can aspire to unless you are blessed with unlimited space and finances. Always buy what you like, and not because of any future investment. While it is true that many of the items released during the original trilogy are now worth many times their original retail, this was precisely because no one knew they would be collectable. Buyers are now much more clued in and few of the products from the last twenty years have seen such levels of appreciation.

Resources such as eBay are a good starting place, but the buyer should always be wary, particularly with older items, where reproductions tend to be rife.

To try and catalogue the complete history of *Star Wars* merchandising would need volumes the size of the *Encyclopaedia Britannica*. This book is not intended as a complete guide, rather as a snapshot of the history of *Star Wars* merchandising with a focus on certain areas, and particularly on those items released during the vintage era. We have had to omit some genres of collecting such as posters, food items and clothing in favour of concentrating on more key products such as the toys and comics. A majority of merchandise over the years originates from America; however, as this book is being published and predominantly sold in the UK, we have decided to give the book a British perspective, with a leaning towards UK editions of items. We have mostly omitted those items released only in foreign territories outside the US and UK.

In recent decades there has a been a tendency towards caricaturing *Star Wars* in merchandising with such products as Lego and Pop Vinyls, as well as cross-pollinations with franchises such as Angry Birds and Muppets. With no disrespect to these lines, we felt they should be classified as a separate genre of *Star Wars* collectable, and have therefore decided to keep the focus of the book on items that interpret *Star Wars* in a realistic way. We have occasionally allowed ourselves to bend these strictures slightly where we felt it necessary, so don't be too surprised if an odd item creeps in that doesn't conform exactly to these guidelines. We have also found that prices on *Star Wars* items are constantly in flux and subject to many factors and so, except in a few instances, we have deliberately avoided giving values.

Whether you're new to the world of *Star Wars* collecting or have been there right from the start, hopefully you will find much to enjoy in this book. Here's to memories of long ago in a toy shop not too far away…

CHAPTER 1

Action Figures, Vehicles and Playsets

Today, an action figure – a toy representation of a character sculpted almost entirely out of plastic with moveable joints – is a common feature in most toy stores. Yet, it is hard to believe that prior to *Star Wars,* such a thing barely existed. There had of course been Action Man in Great Britain and GI Joe in America, but these were essentially boys' dolls. Solidly sculpted figures tended to be either static or rubber with a wire armature. A precursor to the format adopted by the *Star Wars* figures were the Fisher Price Adventure People, launched in 1975. Kenner would actually use the Adventure People figures as the basis for some of the early *Star Wars* prototypes.

Star Wars popularised the pocket action figure, but the size was arrived at out of a matter of necessity. The original intention was for the *Star Wars* figures to be in a 12 inch scale. It was soon realised, however, that the vehicles – a key selling point of the range – would be impractical to produce in this scale.

Kenner did still produce their 12 inch range, but this was as a companion series to a core range of smaller figures measuring 3.75 inches on average. Unfortunately, Kenner had been awarded the *Star Wars* license late in the day and had little time to get products into development for the film's release. They were able to get relatively simple items like board games and jigsaws out in 1977, but the action figures needed a longer lead time. Not wishing to miss out on the lucrative Christmas market, Kenner came up with the idea of an Early Bird package. This contained a cardboard display stand and a mail-in certificate, which gave you the first option on four of the figures: Luke Skywalker, Princess Leia, R2-D2 and Chewbacca.

Early Bird Certificate Package. (Kenner, 1977)

Twelve figures arrived to market in 1978, with Han Solo, C-3PO, Ben (Obi-Wan) Kenobi, Darth Vader, Stormtrooper, Jawa, Tusken Raider and Death Squad Commander joining individual releases of the Early Bird figures.

There are a few variations of the early figures that command high prices today. The Luke, Darth and Obi Wan figures featured a lightsaber, which pushed out the arm. Originally these lightsabers featured thin tips, which extended from the main body of the saber. Unfortunately, these were broken easily, so the saber was modified into one piece with a smaller, fixed tip. The Jawa was noticeably shorter than other characters in the range but sold for the same price. It originally came with a thin plastic vinyl cape, but feeling it didn't offer sufficient value, Kenner replaced the vinyl cape with a cloth one. The vinyl cape Jawa is now one of the most sought-after *Star Wars* figures on the market, with sales upwards of £10,000 recorded on packaged examples. A more common variation is the first Han Solo figure. Shortly after its release, a second, larger-head sculpt was introduced. The small-head Hans continued to be offered for a few years but were eventually phased out, with the larger-head being the more prevalent version today.

British releases of the first twelve action figures. (Palitoy, 1978)

British vinyl cape Jawa figure.
(Palitoy, 1978)

A second series of figures followed in 1979, including the cantina aliens: Greedo, Hammerhead, Walrusman and Snaggletooth. These were first offered through the Sears 1978 catalogue in sets of two shipped loose in a mailer box or packed together in the Cantina Adventure set. Initial shipments from Sears included a variation of Snaggletooth that differs from the later carded release. The rare blue Snaggletooth is much taller and has boots rather than paws. Colours and outfits on these early figures would often differ from what was seen on screen, often as a result of limited reference material.

A late addition to the 1979 range was Boba Fett, trailering his appearance in *The Empire Strikes Back*. Initially offered as a mail-away, the figure was advertised with a firing missile. The missile was dropped prior to production due to a choking incident involving a similar feature on a Mattel *Battlestar Galactica* toy. Prototypes exist of the rocket-firing Fett, but the figure was never released. All production Fetts have the missile fixed in place.

Supplementing the figure range, vehicles and playsets were also produced, including two different Death Stars. In the US, a multi-tiered plastic tower was released, while other territories in the world got a cheaper set made from cardboard.

The rare blue Snaggletooth from Sears' 1978 Cantina Adventure playset.

The second series of action figures introduced a number of background characters to the range, including the corrected Snaggletooth.

With the release of *The Empire Strikes Back*, Kenner began to roll out an increasing amount of product. There were some figure variants such as Lando initially having black eyes and an unpainted mouth, which was later changed to white eyes and mouth, and Princess Leia Bespin with open and turtleneck collars, while Yoda could be found with brown and orange snakes. These variations are much easier to find than those from the first film. New additions to the line included a range of smaller pocket money vehicles called Mini Rigs that didn't actually appear in the movies.

The rarest *Empire* item is the Sears-exclusive Cloud City playset, which, much like the earlier Cantina Adventure set, was just an inexpensive cardboard backdrop used as an incentive to sell some figures.

Return of the Jedi saw by far the largest range of product released to that point. Kenner had trailed the movie, then known as *Revenge of the Jedi,* on some of the latter *Empire* figures and offered an Admiral Ackbar figure as a mail-away. The title was

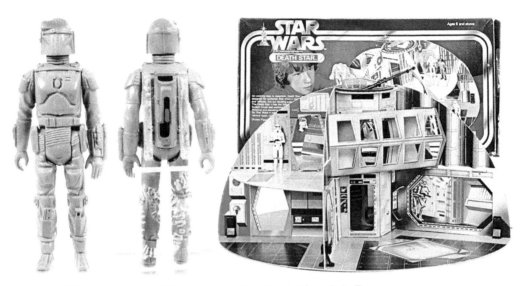

Above left: A rare prototype of the original, unreleased rocket firing Boba Fett.

Above right: Death Star playset. (Palitoy 1978)

Landspeeder. (Kenner, 1978)

Dewback. (Kenner, 1979)

British Palitoy *The Empire Strikes Back* action figures.

changed to *Return of the Jedi* late in the day after Kenner had printed a substantial amount of *Revenge* packaging. No original figures, however, were released on *Revenge* cards, although some uncirculated cardbacks did survive and have found their way into private collections. The *Return of the Jedi* figures tend to be those most commonly found today, particularly many of the aliens. As with many of the earlier figures there are minor differences in paintwork and moulding on several of the Jedi figures due to running changes and different factories used over the years. The most notable variant is Luke Skywalker in Jedi Knight outfit, which was initially released with a blue lightsaber, but this was quickly changed to green to represent the colour used in the movie. Due to its high price point at the time, the large Imperial Shuttle is generally regarded as the rarest of the Jedi toys.

By 1985, and with no further films on the horizon, Kenner rebranded the range as 'The Power of the Force' and figures came packaged with bonus coins. Two of the figures, Anakin Skywalker and Yak Face, were only sold in Power of the Force packaging in Canada, although Anakin had previously been offered in the US as a mail-away. In Europe, all the final figures including Anakin and Yak Face were offered on multilingual *Return of the Jedi* cards omitting the coin. These figures, along with Paploo and Lumat from the Jedi line, are often referred to as the last seventeen and, due to much lower production runs than earlier figures, are now some of the hardest to find.

Kenner also issued short runs for the *Droids and Ewoks* cartoon series, and although further waves of these were planned, these were never released.

Above: A number of collectors' cases were produced to hold the figures, including this Darth Vader model.

Left: The Mini Rigs were small pocket money vehicles that never appeared in the movies.

Although only superficially resembling the onscreen design, this Star Destroyer toy is the only version ever to have been made to accompany the 3.75 inch figures.

Boba Fett's Slave 1 came with a model of Han Solo in Carbonite. This was different to the version that was later released individually.

Cloud City playset. (Kenner, 1980)

Kenner were eager to continue the line beyond the movies and had roughed out a storyline beyond *Return of the Jedi* that would have introduced a new villain called Atha Prime, who comes out of exile and wages war on the Alliance with the aid of his Clone Warriors. They also planned to release various unmade toys from earlier films including a Grand Moff Tarkin figure (Kenner intended Tarkin to have survived the destruction of the Death Star). Various figures and vehicles were at early concept and prototype stages when Lucasfilm declined permission to proceed with the proposed storyline.

With no new movies or toys on the horizon children quickly moved onto other things. Mattel's Masters of the Universe and Hasbro's Transformers both became very popular. In the late 1980s, *Star Wars* toys, once the centrepiece of toy aisles, became bargain bin fodder. Kenner had such an overstock on some items that they were thrown in landfill. Children sold off their loose figures for pennies, and some parents deemed

A surviving *Revenge of the Jedi* card. Despite a large amount being printed, these never made it into stores.

Kenner *Return of the Jedi* action figures.

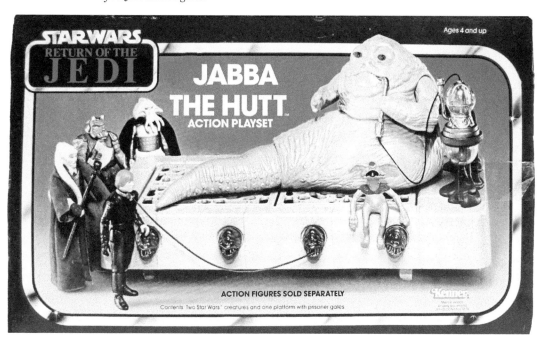

Jabba the Hutt playset. (Kenner, 1983)

Speeder Bike. (Kenner, 1983)

European tri-logo release of Sy Snootles and the Rebo band. In the US the figures were released in window-box packaging.

The Power of the Force branding was never used in the UK; figures were instead released as part of the *Return of the Jedi* line.

them so worthless they threw them out. The same stories abound; the truth is that few had forward thinking or realised that the time for these toys would come again.

By the nineties, the children who had grown up with the original films were coming of age and now had a disposable income. Slowly but surely a *Star Wars* collectors market began to emerge as fans sought to reacquire the toys they used to own.

Quick to establish themselves at the top of many collectors' lists were the vinyl cape Jawa, blue Snaggletooth and the final last seventeen figures. The rarest *Star Wars* figure of all, however, turned out to be one few were aware of. In the late 1980s, Glasslite of Brazil belatedly released the *Droids and Ewoks* animated figures, including Vlix, a character from the unreleased second *Droids* wave. Vlix now commands insane sums, with a sale of £12,000 being recorded on a packaged example in 2016.

Above left: Imperial Shuttle. (Kenner, 1984)

Above right: Yak Face was never released in the US but received wide distribution across Europe.

  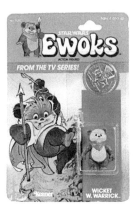 

Droids and Ewoks animated series figures, these were never released in the UK.

Most children buying a figure would not have given a second thought to ripping it from its packaging, but as *Star Wars* collecting took off, many collectors began to seek out figures still sealed on their original cards. The cards for the first *Star Wars* movie became the most desirable. Kenner had kept most figures in production through to *Return of the Jedi*, while a limited selection of older figures appeared in the Power of the Force line. There were also many changes to the reverse of the cards. Initial backs featured pictures of twelve characters, which was then updated as new characters were added. The original cards, dubbed 12-backs, are now some of the most highly prized. Character photos were sometimes changed on the cards, and mail-in stickers and promotions were often added. A large amount of card variants therefore exist for many of the characters, with varying degrees of rarity.

While Kenner controlled US and Canadian distribution, overseas the figures were handled by other companies, including Palitoy in the UK. To streamline European distribution, multilingual cards referred to as tri-logos were introduced in the latter years of the range. These featured the *Return of the Jedi* logo three times in English, French and Spanish.

While vintage carded figures are becoming harder to find, loose figures tend to be more plentiful. Due to their having been handled, condition can be extremely variable and weapons may have been lost.

It is now forty years since the original *Star Wars* figures first appeared, and with an influx of new collectors in recent years, demand for these vintage items continues to be on the rise.

As *Star Wars* became coveted by collectors, Kenner soon realised that there was a market for new figures. Since the last figures had been released in 1985, the only comparable product had been a series of bendable figures from Just Toys aptly called *Star Wars* Bend Ems. After a decade-long break, Kenner, now a subsidiary of its old rival Hasbro, began issuing new figures in 1995.

Kenner retained the classic 3.75 inch scale and The Power of the Force subtitle was revived. Wrestling figures were popular at the time and Kenner thought kids would respond well to figures in action stances with a more muscular look. The range expanded rapidly and within the first few years had eclipsed the ninety-six figures issued during the vintage run. As well as updating many old figures, the range also included characters never before released such as Grand Moff Tarkin and the Rebel Fleet Trooper. Vehicles were also issued to accompany the figures, although a majority reused old vintage toolings.

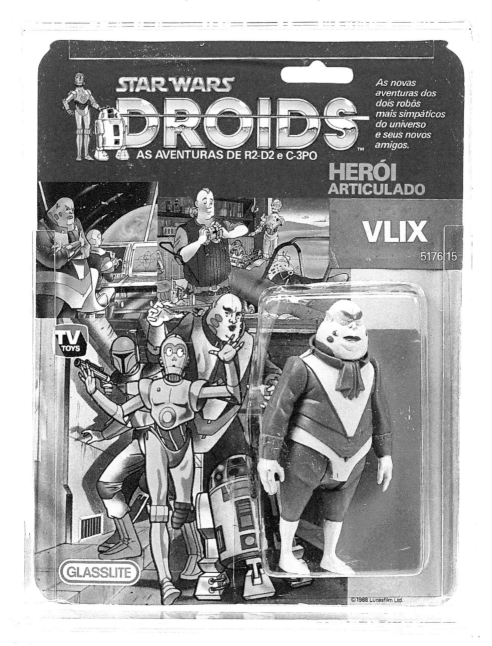

Vlix, the rarest *Star Wars* figure of all, was only available in Brazil.

The Power of the Force line also incorporated two short sublines – Shadows of the Empire, based on the 1996 multimedia event, and the Expanded Universe, which covered comics, books, video games and concept designs. Various bonus pack-ins including freeze frame action slides were introduced with later figures in the run. The revived Power of the Force was be the final *Star Wars* line released under the Kenner

Several of the European tri-logo figures featured different imagery on the cards.

Just Toys' *Star Wars* Bend Ems filled a void at a time when there were no new action figures on the market.

label; later waves were released under Hasbro branding and the Kenner name would only appear in future on retro-themed products.

The arrival of *Star Wars: Episode 1* was heralded by two sneak preview items – a mail-away Mace Windu figure and a Battle Droid with STAP, which could be bought in stores. The main *Episode 1* figures came with a Commtech chip – a new pack-in that

After a break of ten years, *Star Wars* figures returned with the Power of the Force line in 1995.

appeared to make the figures talk when used with the Commtech reader, which could be purchased separately.

While in the past the look of the *Star Wars* lines had been relatively uniform and consistent, Hasbro would soon begin rebranding the range and changing the packaging design on a regular basis. Power of the Jedi and the Original Trilogy Collection filled the void between *Episode 1* and *Episode 3*, while *Attack of the Clones* figures appeared in packaging simply titled *Star Wars* alongside other characters from the saga. Following the end of the prequel trilogy lines with *Revenge of the Sith*, future collections would encompass the entirety of the saga and bonus pack-ins began to feature once more. The Saga Collection introduced bonus mini holograms, while the 30th Anniversary Collection saw the return of collector's coins and Build a Droid parts were offered in the Legacy Collection. After releasing several short runs of new figures on reproductions of the original vintage cards, many fans got their wish when the concept was revived for a full line appropriately titled the Vintage Collection, which ran for two years and incorporated 115 figures.

The late 2000s saw the debut of the *Clone Wars* animated movie and series and a tie in line of figures. There had, in fact, already been two previous series of *Clone Wars* figures – one with Hasbro designs in 2003, and then animated-style figures in 2004 and 2005 based on the designs from the Cartoon Network shorts. The release of *The Phantom Menace* in 3D continued to keep *Star Wars* in the limelight and the accompanying figure line came in Darth Maul-themed packaging. 3D versions of *Attack of the Clones* and *Revenge of the Sith* were intended to follow but Disney dropped the

Many of the *Star Wars: Episode 1* figures were widely discounted after release, but some of the latter figures in the line are rare.

Originally intended to be part of the Power of the Force and *Episode 1* lines, figures were instead released as part of a new range titled Power of the Jedi.

films following their purchase of Lucasfilm. Hasbro had little choice but to release toys planned for both movies. A short run of figures in Yoda-branded packaging for *Attack of the Clones* were only released outside the US, while the *Revenge of the Sith* range featuring Darth Vader-themed cards received a wider release.

This time of uncertainty for the range also saw Hasbro scrap plans to revive the Legacy Collection, partway through production. Only a set of six figures exclusive to Amazon and a small amount of stock of Waves 1 and 2 were ever released in this packaging style. Planned Legacy Collection figures were instead released under Hasbro's collector-focused Black Series branding.

In recent years, and now under the aegis of Disney, the Hasbro *Star Wars* figure range has once more resumed a consistency. Figures and vehicles continue to be released for the *Rebels* animated series and each of the new theatrical movies. More collector-orientated 3.75 inch figures are still offered as part of the Black Series and the Vintage Collection is currently slated to return in 2018.

As well as the ongoing core 3.75 inch figure collections, there have also been a number of companion products over the years, including greatest hits waves, deluxe sets, comic packs, multipacks, figure and vehicle sets and even carry cases.

The early 2000s saw a wide variety of packaging designs used on the figures.

Revenge of the Sith was the largest figure range for any *Star Wars* movie to date, with over sixty figures being released.

It is now approaching twenty-five years since the 1990s relaunch of *Star Wars* figures and the range has seen many ups and downs in popularity and collectability during that time. The Power of the Force and prequel movie figures were produced in such numbers that many are still commonly available today. From 2006 onwards, with no live action films in the pipeline, production numbers and interest steadily declined and

During the late 2000s figures became increasingly detailed and many never-before-released characters were introduced to the range.

Hasbro regularly revised the packaging to tie in with big *Star Wars* events such as the *Clone Wars* animated series, the *Episode 1* 3D release and the ultimately cancelled 3D versions of *Episode 2* and *3*.

While the Vintage Collection is often seen as the pinnacle of the modern *Star Wars* range, follow on collector-orientated lines failed to ignite the same interest.

figures from the later lines are now the hardest to find. Modern-age rarities include Darth Revan (a popular video game character), Jacen and Jaina Solo (the twins of Han and Leia from the books) and Darth Sidious (from the Clone Wars). A comic pack set containing Uliq Qel Droma and Exar Kun from *Tales of the Jedi* is the hardest-to-find modern release, often fetching several hundred pounds in online auctions.

While the 3.75 inch range is undoubtedly the most prolific, it should not be forgotten that there have been other scales of action figure. Kenner debuted a 12 inch range in 1978 with ten characters from the first movie. Boba Fett was later released ahead of his appearance in *The Empire Strikes Back,* and while further *Empire* figures were prototyped, only an IG-88 saw release. In the UK, eight of the figures were first released through Denys Fisher before their parent company Palitoy took over the range.

Kenner stopped production on the 12 inch range as the 3.75 inch figures were such a runaway success and they wished to plough all their resources into the smaller scale. However, the 12 inch format would enjoy a new lease of life in the nineties, with Hasbro issuing over 100 figures between 1996 and 2005. With the 12 inch style of action figure being increasingly marketed as a high-end collectable, Sideshow Collectibles took over the license and introduced a more detailed and accurate line of figures. Over the years, Sideshow have also issued various beasts and dioramas to accompany the figures.

Above: With the yearly release rate of new movies, the Disney *Star Wars* figure lines represent a sparser selection of characters than in the past.

Below left: 30th Anniversary Collection Darth Revan. (Hasbro, 2007)

Below right: : The Uliq Qel Droma and Exar Kun comic pack set is the rarest modern *Star Wars* release.

Sideshow have partnered with the Hong Kong company Hot Toys on several of their releases. Hot Toys, renowned for their outstanding character likenesses, also produce their own *Star Wars* range and generally handle new movie figures along with updated versions of old favourites, while Sideshow continue to release characters from the older films.

Star Wars 12 inch figures are not as widely collected as the 3.75 inch scale, but still have a strong following. The Vintage dolls are the most sought after, particularly in good boxed condition. There is less of a following for Hasbro releases from the

The Legacy Collection Jacen and Jaina Solo. (Hasbro, 2009)

1990s and 2000s, which can be picked up relatively cheaply. Many collectors opt for the superior versions since put out by Sideshow and Hot Toys. These are produced in considerably lower quantities than the Hasbro figures, and many of the older Sideshow figures are becoming hard to find.

While *Star Wars* led the industry for a time with the 3.75 inch scale, by the nineties *Star Wars* was one of the few toy lines still using the size. Hasbro realised that there was a demand for bigger and more detailed figures and over the years has had various attempts at introducing a larger scale, including the short-lived Epic Force and Mega Action lines. *Star Wars* Unleashed, a series of stylised figurines with diorama bases, was to prove more popular, with over thirty releases. It has only been in recent years that Hasbro has finally achieved success in the larger scale with super articulated 6 inch figures being released under the Black Series banner. The new line has proven a serious rival to the 3.75 inch range and over eighty figures have so far been released, along with various beasts and vehicles. Many of the earlier figures are already highly sought after.

Other ranges that may be of interest to *Star Wars* figure collectors include a range of 18 inch talking figures from Diamond Select and various scales of oversized vinyl figures from Jakks Pacific, as well as die-cast figures and 11 inch dolls released as part of the Disney Store's *Star Wars* Elite range.

Unlike the 1980s where Kenner controlled all the figure rights, the license is now split among various companies, and collectors these days are much less likely to be completists than in the past when there were fewer lines to follow.

While *Star Wars* continues to be popular, it is likely that there will always be figures of the characters. While there have been challenges to its supremacy, and different scales will surely come and go, it is likely 3.75 inches will continue to be the size most associated with *Star Wars*.

Above: The original *Star Wars* 12 inch line was short-lived but the figures were some of the first items to become collectable.

Left: Sideshow Collectibles and Hot Toys now produce their 12 inch figures specifically for the collectors' market.

The revival of the *Star Wars* 12 inch line was to prove much longer lived than the vintage dolls.

The Black Series line is continually expanding and in recent years has overtaken the 3.75 inch range in popularity.

CHAPTER 2

Toys, Models and Games

When talking about *Star Wars* toys, it is easy to concentrate purely on the action figures, but there have been many other types of toys released for the films.

Kenner's initial rollout of product concentrated on traditional items such as jigsaws and board games, which could be quickly and cheaply manufactured.

Three board games were released for the first movie, including Escape from the Death Star, Destroy Death Star and the Adventures of R2-D2. In the UK, a different battery-operated Destroy Death Star game was issued by Palitoy. *The Empire Strikes Back* saw Kenner issue two further games: the Hoth Ice Planet Adventure Game and Yoda the Jedi Master. The license then moved to General Mills' Parker Brothers division, with *Star Wars*: The Ultimate Space Adventure Game and Battle at Sarlacc's Pit, along with two Ewok-themed games.

Kenner also produced two electronic games: the Electronic Laser Battle Game and the Electronic Battle Command Game. There was also the X-Wing Ace's Target Game, which was basically a redressed version of an old Kenner shooting game called Aerial Aces.

In 1987 a company called West End Games acquired the *Star Wars* license, and as well as releasing four board games, they also introduced the *Star Wars* roleplaying game. This consisted of sourcebooks and adventure supplements, along with a series of white metal miniatures. The *Star Wars* roleplaying game is notable for coining many names and establishing background information that became part of established *Star Wars* lore.

Various board games released during the 1970s and 1980s.

In the UK Palitoy released a different version of the Destroy Death Star Game.

The *Star Wars* Electronic Battle Command Game was a variation on the popular Battleship game.

West End Games, producers of the *Star Wars* roleplaying game, were one of the few companies offering *Star Wars* product in the late 1980s.

Waddingtons released several photographic puzzles for *Star Wars* and *Return of the Jedi* but didn't issue any jigsaws for *The Empire Strikes Back*.

Kenner and Craftmaster issued *Star Wars* and Jedi jigsaws in America. In the UK the license was awarded to Waddingtons, who produced four photographic jigsaws for the first movie and two featuring the Kenner action figures. Waddingtons offered another four jigsaws for *Return of the Jedi*, which came with a fold-out poster of the puzzle image. Their final *Star Wars* offerings were four *Ewoks* animated series jigsaws.

The vintage *Star Wars* die-cast range is now highly sought after.

A big selling point for *Star Wars* was the spaceships, and a range of die-cast and plastic models of the more popular vehicles were produced by Kenner. An X-Wing, TIE Fighter, Landspeeder and Darth Vader's TIE Fighter came packaged on blister cards, while the larger *Millennium Falcon*, Y-Wing and Imperial Cruiser came in boxes. The Imperial Cruiser was actually an early name for the Star Destroyer, before Lucasfilm decided on a more sinister moniker for the Empire's wedge-shaped starships. Further releases for *The Empire Strikes Back* included carded releases of a Snowspeeder, *Slave 1* and Twin-Pod Cloud Car, along with a boxed TIE Bomber. The die-casts were one of several casualties of Kenner's *Return of the Jedi* line, which saw most of their attention directed towards the 3.75 inch figure range. In the UK, Palitoy only offered the vehicles for the first film. Due to a limited release, the TIE Bomber is the hardest to find in the range.

Kenner had high hopes for another smaller scale series: the *Star Wars* Micro Collection, which launched in 1982. The range comprised playsets representing sections of various *Star Wars* environments, which came with small die-cast figurines. Two Death Star sets, four Hoth and three Bespin sets were produced. Each set was designed to connect to another in the same series. The individual sets were also collected together and sold in larger World sets. There were several vehicles, including an X-Wing and a TIE Fighter. The *Millennium Falcon* was produced as a Sears exclusive while the Snowspeeder could only be bought through J. C. Penney. A free Build Your Armies set comprising three Hoth Rebel Soldiers and three Snowtroopers could also be sent away for. Unfortunately, the Micro Collection did not perform as well as Kenner hoped, and despite further sets having been prototyped, the range was quickly cancelled.

The *Star Wars* Micro Collection was an ambitious idea that failed to take off with kids.

Action Masters were the first new *Star Wars* products issued by Kenner since the 1980s.

Just prior to relaunching the 3.75 inch action figure line in the 1990s, Kenner had another attempt at the die-cast format. Action Masters was a series of 2.5-inch-tall metal figurines that also incorporated other licensed properties including *Terminator 2* and *Aliens*. The die-casts were released both individually and in multipacks and came with trading cards of the characters. Certain characters weren't sold individually and could only be found in the multipacks. A mail-in gold C-3PO figurine was offered, which differed from the regular version.

A prolific *Star Wars* toy range of the nineties was the Micro Machines line from Galoob toys. These were small plastic vehicles measuring around 1–2 inches that were initially sold in sets of three, each being themed around one of the films. The Micro Machines proved extremely popular and the range of products expanded rapidly. Environment playsets were introduced, which included mini plastic figurines, and the figurines were also made available in blister packs. As well as covering the movies, Galoob also issued figure and ship packs based on *Shadows of the Empire* and some of the novels.

The *Star Wars* Micro Machines brand was soon extended to cover various other scales and ranges. The X-Ray Fleet was a series of models rendered in transparent plastic, which allowed you to see the ships' workings. There was a range of die-cast models and a line of larger ships featuring moveable parts called Action Fleet. The

Above and overleaf: Star Wars Micro Machines were to prove one of the most popular *Star Wars* toy lines in the 1990s.

Action Fleet vehicles came boxed with two semi-poseable mini figures. The Action Fleet range grew to incorporate playsets, the Series Alpha subline, which paired a vehicle with a smaller concept design version, and battle packs that contained figures along with a beast or small vehicle.

During the nineties, the *Star Wars* Micro Machines range had proven itself somewhat of a rival to Kenner/Hasbro's revived action figure line. Soon, however, both properties were under one roof, when Hasbro acquired Galoob in 1998. The first Micro Machines carrying joint Hasbro/Galoob branding were released for *Star Wars: Episode 1* with a Gian Speeder and Theed Palace preview set released ahead of the film. New products introduced for *Episode 1* included build-your-own Podracers, mini scenes and Podracer launchers.

Star Wars: Episode 1 marked the last regular Micro Machine offerings, although Hasbro would continue to revive the name occasionally with Action Fleet vehicles for *Attack of the Clones* and mini figures and vehicles for *Revenge of the Sith* and *The Force Awakens*.

The Micro Machines label was also attached to a die-cast range called Titanium, featuring pocket-sized renditions of the ships. One of Hasbro's more successful lines, Titanium featured over 150 releases.

Currently, few Micro Machines sets sell for particularly high prices on the aftermarket. Exceptions to the rule, however, are the Action Fleet E-Wing and TIE Defender ships, both of which are based on Expanded Universe designs.

Another notable but short-lived range of *Star Wars* vehicles was Kenner's Collector Fleet in the 1990s. This featured replicas of the larger ships that were impractical to produce in scale with the 3.75 inch action figures. The vehicles featured light and sound effects and came with a display stand. The initial releases of the Rebel Blockade Runner and an Imperial Star Destroyer were later followed by a Super Star Destroyer.

A perennially popular product is the buildable model kit and there have been many *Star Wars* releases over the years mainly concentrating on the saga's vehicles. MPC, another subsidiary of General Mills, were the first to issue kits with Luke's X-Wing,

The Super Star Destroyer is the scarcest of the three *Star Wars* Collector Fleet vehicles.

Airfix issued *Star Wars* kits for the UK market.

Screamin released a range of vinyl character kits during the 1990s.

Darth Vader's TIE Fighter, the *Millennium Falcon* and figural kits of R2-D2, C-3PO and Darth Vader being released for the first film. *The Empire Strikes Back* saw a more expansive range of models including snap-fix environment dioramas. *Return of the Jedi* added two new sub ranges: Structors, kits that actually walked, and Mirra-kits, where half of the vehicle was supplied and a mirror would appear to make the ship complete. It was during *Return of the Jedi* that MPC became known as MPC/Ertl. In the UK the kits for the first film were initially released by Denys Fisher, with Airfix taking over distribution from *The Empire Strikes Back*.

After a break of several years, AMT/Ertl, as they were now known, began reissuing their *Star Wars* kits from 1989, with new kits being added during the nineties. The kits for *Episode 1* were to be AMT/Ertl's final *Star Wars* releases. Revell picked up the model kit license for *Revenge of the Sith* and have continued to release kits to the present.

Large vinyl character kits were a popular product in the early nineties and Screamin were at the forefront of the market. The company began issuing *Star Wars* models from 1993 and produced nine 1/4 scale kits along with five kits in a smaller 1/6 scale.

Star Wars kits are generally considered more valuable if they are unmade and are still sealed in their original packaging.

Star Wars toys have offered many roleplay opportunities over the years for children. Kenner offered budding junior rebels the option of the laser pistol or the three-position laser rifle. The laser pistol was released in packaging for all three original movies, while the three-position rifle was only released for the first movie, but was later retooled and sold as the electronic laser rifle for *The Empire Strikes Back*. Both items were re-released in the 1990s but were rendered in bright non-movie colours to comply with

Star Wars Laser Pistol. (Kenner, 1978)

Star Wars Three Position Laser Rifle. (Palitoy, 1979)

The earliest toy lightsaber was this inflatable version.

Biker Scout Laser Pistol.
(Kenner, 1983)

Kenner released various plush Ewoks in both small and large sizes.

new laws over the marketing of toy guns. A scarcer 1980s roleplay item was the Biker Scout laser pistol from *Return of the Jedi*.

While the lightsaber is undoubtedly the most iconic of all *Star Wars* weapons, it took a while for Kenner to hit on a successful design. An early 1978 version featured an inflatable blade, before a solid tube design was introduced for *The Empire Strikes Back*. Known as the Force Saber, these were sold loose in dumpbins and came in yellow and red colours, with green later being added for *Return of the Jedi*. Another lightsaber design accompanied the *Star Wars* Droids toy range, featuring a battery-operated extending blade.

The debut of the teddy-bear-like Ewoks in *Return of the Jedi* resulted in the obvious merchandising tie-in of plush versions. There were four larger Ewoks – Wicket, Paploo, Princess Knessa and Latara – along with six smaller Woklings. A fifth large Ewok called Zephee was depicted on tags, but was never released.

Kenner have also released one-off toys tied into various characters. R2-D2 was available as both a radio-control version and also a talking model from Palitoy in the UK, which, alongside the characteristic bleeps and bloops, strangely had the character saying 'I am R2-D2' in English. Yoda was also released as a one-piece rubber hand puppet.

One of Kenner's more obscure lines were the *Star Wars* Bop Bags – inflatable punch bags that came in four designs: Chewbacca, Vader, R2-D2 and Jawa (with perhaps all

Above left: Surprisingly, given his popularity, this Yoda puppet was one of the few toys produced for the character during the 1980s.

Above right: Radio Controlled R2-D2. (Palitoy, 1979)

Left: R2-D2 Inflatable Bop Bag. (Kenner, 1978)

Luke Skywalker AM Headset Radio. (Kenner, 1978)

Play-Doh Adventure Modelling set. (Palitoy, 1978)

but one of the character choices undeserving of the inevitable battering they would receive from diminutive fists). Some early Kenner Star Wars items adapted pre-existing products, such as Luke Skywalker's AM Radio headset, which had previously been marketed as a Six Million Dollar Man toy.

Kenner also introduced a Star Wars version of their popular children's modelling toy Play Doh. Six sets were released in total during the vintage era.

In more recent times there has been further cross-pollination of brands with *Star Wars* versions of everything from Monopoly to Transformers. The amount of toys and games based on the saga is now so vast that there surely can't be many popular children's products for which a *Star Wars* version doesn't currently exist.

CHAPTER 3

Collectables

While many *Star Wars* items are today targeted specifically at the collector's base, it should be remembered that in the early days there were barely any products that would qualify as collectable. Merchandise was mass produced and aimed primarily at children. There was little concept of any longevity or that *Star Wars* would continue to be collected into adulthood.

It was only when *Star Wars* turned ten years old in 1987 that a collectables market slowly began to emerge. To celebrate the tenth anniversary, a set of six collector's coins were released by Rarities mint. The coins came in four varieties: one ounce silver, five ounce silver, quarter ounce gold and one ounce gold. The prices for each type were progressively more expensive, with the one ounce gold coins retailing for a staggering $1,000 each.

Darth Vader and Ben Kenobi Collector's Coin. (Rarities Mint, 1988)

Star Wars collector's plates from the Hamilton Collection.

The same year also saw the release of a series of collector's plates from the Hamilton Collection. Hamilton continued to issue further plates through the 1990s.

The nineties saw an increasing number of products aimed squarely at the dedicated collector, many of which were marketed as limited editions.

Illusive Concepts, a company mainly known for making masks, produced several *Star Wars* collectables. The most notable offerings were life-size replicas of Yoda and of Han Solo frozen in Carbonite. There was also a series of maquettes including a 1/1 scale representation of Chewbacca's head along with a life-size bust of the unmasked Darth Vader.

A name commonly found on *Star Wars* products in the nineties was Applause, who produced a range of giftware. They did, however, venture into the collectable market with various diorama pieces, many featuring a faux antique finish. To tie in with the release of *Star Wars: Episode 1*, Applause also released a series of 6-inch-tall resin character statues.

Perhaps the closest for many collectors to taking the movie home is owning a prop replica. In 1996, Icons were the first to issue screen-accurate reproductions of the Luke Skywalker, Darth Vader and Obi Wan lightsaber hilts along with X-Wing and TIE Fighter models.

In 2001 the prop replica license passed to Master Replicas, who would release a much more extensive line. As well as a range of lightsaber hilts, they also issued blasters and various other replicas. Full-size reproduction helmets were produced, including many of the Clone Troopers. Some of their more impressive items were their replicas of the original model filming miniatures. A number of the Master Replicas items were produced as signature editions and came with a special plaque signed by a cast member. While these items were aimed at the higher end of the market, Master Replicas also produced various items at a more affordable price point. There was a

Above left: Life-size Yoda. (Illusive Concepts, 1995)

Above right: Rancor statue. (Applause, 1997)

range of lightsabers with light and sound titled Force FX, which featured metal hilts with a polypropylene blade attached. The Force FX sabers would prove extremely popular, and following the expiration of Master Replica's license, Hasbro would take over the Force FX brand. Also released was a miniature line with lightsaber hilts at .45 scale and blasters at .33 scale, along with a range of scaled helmets.

EFX took on the *Star Wars* license in 2008 and have produced further ships, lightsabers and helmets, including some based on Ralph McQuarrie concept designs.

Above and overleaf: Various prop reproductions from Master Replicas.

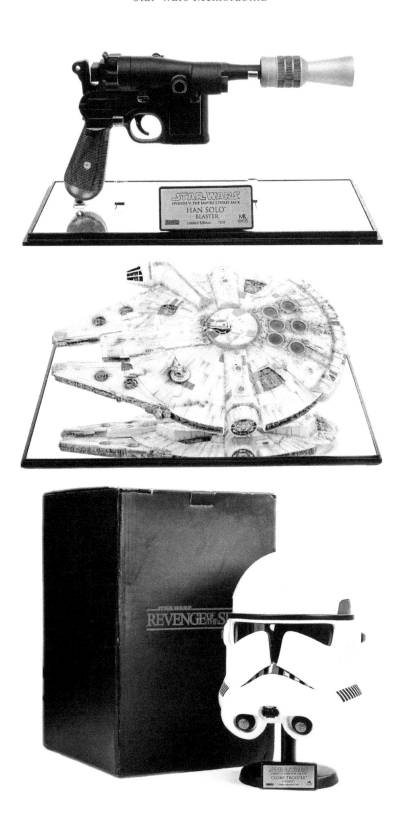

A popular collectable over the past couple of decades is the bust – a statue usually representing the upper torso of a character. Legends in 3 Dimensions issued several *Star Wars* characters in a 9 inch scale in the nineties. Gentle Giant introduced a smaller scale of around 6 inches, dubbed the mini bust, when they debuted their range in 2002.

The first busts were based on *Attack of the Clones* but the line soon expanded to cover various classic characters. Over the last sixteen years, Gentle Giant have issued over 150 busts. The line has also incorporated characters from the *Clone Wars* and Expanded Universe along with Ralph McQuarrie concept designs. Early busts were sculpted without arms, but the armless design was soon phased out in favour of a full representation of the upper body. Each bust is a limited edition, although edition sizes have varied greatly from a low of 400 pieces to a massive 20,000. The range has included regular exclusive releases that can only be obtained by joining Gentle Giant's Premier Guild collector's club.

In addition to the mini busts, Gentle Giant have also issued two other scales of armless busts both under the *Star Wars* Classics label. There have also been statues in a number of scales including 12 inch character figurines and diorama pieces. Animated maquettes were produced for the *Clone Wars* and *Rebels* along with original designs for classic characters in that style. Life-size monument editions have also been made available of the Yoda and Princess Leia maquettes.

In recent years Gentle Giant have begun issuing *Star Wars* Jumbo figures. These are reproductions of the original 3.75 inch vintage figures but scaled up to 12 inches. Figures come in clamshell packaging replicating the original vintage cards. They have also released various companion pieces, including the Wampa, the Dianoga creature and jumbo versions of the Early Bird and Cantina adventure sets. For collectors with deep pockets, a few of the figures have been issued in the life-size monument scale.

Another major player in the *Star Wars* collectables market over the last decade is Sideshow Collectibles. As well as producing their 1/6 range of action figures,

Various mini busts from
Gentle Giant studios.

Gentle Giant's *Star Wars* Jumbo range brings the classic Kenner figures back to life in a larger 12 inch scale.

Sideshow has also produced a number of high-end collectables. Their first *Star Wars* products were a range of Premium Format figures. These are a hybrid of statue and doll comprising real fabric components over a mainly polystone body. The figures are rendered in 1/4 scale and some of the figures incorporate electronic features such as illuminating lightsabers. Over forty figures have been issued to date.

Sideshow have also produced two series of busts. The first was a highly detailed range in 1/1 scale, which included fabric components. The other was a series of Legendary busts measuring approximately 17 inches featuring the head and a section of the torso. The Legendary label also incorporated a series of figures similar in concept to the premium format but at ½ scale with a retail of around £2,000.

There have also been more traditional statues, including a range of dioramas replicating key scenes from the films, and the Mythos line of statues featuring more artistic interpretations of characters. Recently, Sideshow have begun issuing statues based on the Ralph McQuarrie concept designs.

For collectors who would like to go large, Sideshow have also produced several life-size figures, but these are accompanied by a comparably large retail price in the £7,000 to £9,000 range.

Over the last twenty-five years, the *Star Wars* collectors market has seen quite a few changes, and many of the early licensees have long since vanished into history. Despite being marketed as collectables, it shouldn't always be assumed that limited edition necessarily equates to an investment. The future collectability of an item can depend on many factors, and with many items that are expensive to begin with, it doesn't always follow that prices will rise further.

While there is little demand today for many of the nineties collectables, prop replica items are always popular, and given the longevity of their lines Sideshow and Gentle Giant pieces continue to have a solid collectors base.

Although *Star Wars* collectables are not the cheapest product on the market, it's fair to say they are some of the most impressive and aesthetically pleasing items available, making a good focal point for any collection.

Right: Luke Skywalker, Jedi Knight premium format figure. (Sideshow, 2010)

Below: Princess Leia *v.* Jabba the Hutt statue. (Sideshow, 2010)

CHAPTER 4

Books

One of the few items to predate the release of *Star Wars* was the novelisation of the movie. Released by Ballantine in November 1976, the book played a major part in generating buzz for the upcoming film. The novel was credited to George Lucas but was actually ghost-written by Alan Dean Foster. Numerous editions have been printed over the years and the title is estimated to have sold at least 3.5 million copies. In the UK, the paperback was issued by Sphere in 1977.

Alan Dean Foster's contract for the novelisation also called for a sequel book. *Splinter of the Mind's Eye* was published in 1978 by Del Rey in the US and Sphere in the UK. The book was commissioned with the possibility that it could be used as the basis for a low-budget sequel, if *Star Wars* was to prove only a modest success. This explains why the book is almost entirely set on the fog-shrouded planet of Mimban.

Han Solo would become the star of a trilogy of novels comprising *Han Solo at Stars' End*, *Han Solo's Revenge* and *Han Solo and the Lost Legacy*, all written by

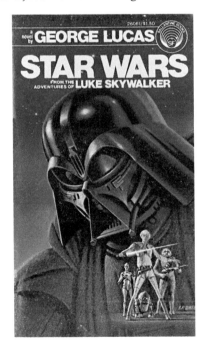

Above left: The 1976 Ballantine novelisation of *Star Wars* featured cover art by Ralph McQuarrie.

Above right: *Splinter of the Mind's Eye* was the first original *Star Wars* novel.

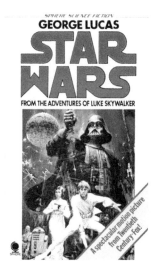  

British paperback novelisations of the original films.

Brian Daley. The books were not allowed to feature recognisable *Star Wars* elements such as the Empire, so Daley created another corrupt regime to pit against Han and Chewie – the Corporate Sector Authority. *Han Solo at Stars' End* was also adapted as a newspaper strip, which was later collected as a miniseries by Dark Horse comics.

Readers of these early spin-off novels would become familiar with a phrase used on the cover – 'From the Adventures of Luke Skywalker' – and the absence of the words '*Star Wars*' in the title. It is often forgotten that in these early years *Star Wars* was purely the name of the first film, and not necessarily a banner that would be applied to any further entries in the canon. Early scripts for the first movie had in fact been titled 'Adventures of the Starkiller, Episode 1: The Star Wars'.

The Empire Strikes Back was novelised by Donald F. Glut. Glut was a classmate of Lucas' from film school and had previously turned down the opportunity to novelise the first movie. James Khan handled the novelisation of *Return of the Jedi*, which was issued as a paperback in the UK by Futura. Both the *Empire* and *Jedi* novels were also available as shortened junior versions and illustrated editions.

The next spin-off novels centred on the exploits of Lando Calrissian. Set before the events of the movies when he owned the *Millennium Falcon*, Lando is accompanied on his adventures by a droid co-pilot, Vuffi Raa. Three novels were released, all by L. Neil Smith, including *Lando Calrissian and the Mindharp of Sharu*, *Lando Calrissian and the Flamewind of Oseon* and *Lando Calrissian and the Starcave of Thonboka*. As with the Solo novels, Smith was not allowed to use any elements from the movies other than Lando and the *Falcon*, so the adventures took place in another region of the galaxy called the Centrality. The Lando books were not initially released in the UK, but Boxtree eventually put out British printings in the nineties.

Alongside the mass market paperbacks, the 1970s and 1980s books also received hardback printings intended for supply to libraries as well as book club editions.

The 1990s was to herald a new era for *Star Wars* publishing. Bantam kicked off a new trilogy of books in 1991 with *Heir to the Empire* by Timothy Zahn. Set five years after the events of *Return of the Jedi*, a New Republic has been formed and the Empire driven to the distant reaches of the galaxy. Han and Leia are married and expecting

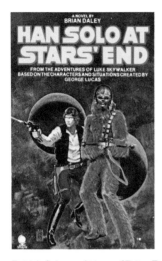

British Sphere editions of Brian Daley's Han Solo Trilogy.

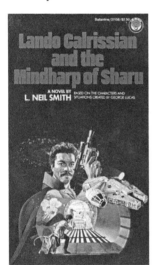

Original US editions of L. Neil Smith's Lando Calrissian Trilogy.

twins; meanwhile, an Imperial Warlord – Grand Admiral Thrawn – begins to gather his forces for an attack. *Heir to the Empire* is a milestone in *Star Wars* history and played a large part in reigniting interest in the saga after the lull of the late eighties. Many aspects of the novel have endured over the decades, with the Imperial capital Coruscant becoming a feature of the prequel films and Grand Admiral Thrawn appearing in the *Rebels* television show. Two further novels followed in the trilogy: *Dark Force Rising* in 1992 and *The Last Command* in 1993. Following the success of these initial books, Bantam continued to release several *Star Wars* novels a year.

Although a majority of the novels were set in the post *Return of the Jedi* era, as the range expanded books would venture further back into the *Star Wars* timeline. The novel for the 1996 multimedia event *Shadows of the Empire* bridged the gap between *Empire* and *Jedi*, while A. C. Crispin's Han Solo Trilogy focused on events before *A New Hope*. Spin-off ranges were also introduced including the X-Wing books and the Tales Anthology series.

Timothy Zahn's *Heir to the Empire* novel sparked a resurgence of interest in *Star Wars*.

As the nineties drew to a close, and with new movies on the horizon, Bantam's license came to an end.

The rights to original *Star Wars* fiction returned to the original license holders, Del Rey – part of the Random House group. In the UK a majority of the books would be published under Random House's Arrow imprint. Their first offering was the novelisation of *Episode 1: The Phantom Menace*, which was adapted by renowned fantasy novelist Terry Brooks. *Attack of the Clones* would later be novelised by R. A. Salvatore, while Matthew Stover penned *Revenge of the Sith*.

Del Rey launched an ongoing series entitled *The New Jedi Order*, set twenty-one years after the events of *Jedi*. The series debuted with *Vector Prime* by R. A. Salvatore, which saw a new threat to the republic as the galaxy is invaded by an alien race called the Yuuzhan Vong. Controversially, the book featured the death of Chewbacca. The New Jedi Order books wrapped up with *The Unifying Force* by James Luceno and two further series followed: *Legacy of the Force* and *Fate of the Jedi*. The 2013 release of *Star Wars Crucible* by Troy Denning effectively marked the end of an era; this was the last chronological entry in the future *Star Wars* timeline, which stretched back to 1991's *Heir to the Empire*.

The 2012 purchase of Lucasfilm by Walt Disney studios and plans for new films meant the books represented somewhat of a roadblock. The novels had given the main characters complex histories and relationships. To try and fit new films into the tangled web that the *Star Wars* Expanded Universe had become was not an option Lucasfilm wished to pursue. All previous spin-off fiction was now not to be regarded as part of official continuity, and future novels would be coordinated by the Lucasfilm Story Group and become part of a new Expanded Universe. The first book to be part of this initiative was *A New Dawn* by

Above and opposite: The vast library of *Star Wars* novels covers all aspects of the saga.

John Jackson Miller – a prequel to the *Star Wars Rebels* television show. Further novels have abandoned the forward narrative of the past with predominantly standalone books based around various aspects of the saga. In 2015 Alan Dean Foster once again returned to the world of *Star Wars* with the novelisation for *The Force Awakens*.

As well as the traditional novels, there has also been a separate strand of fiction targeted at younger readers. During the 1970s and 1980s, these tended to be simplistic picture books and read-along storybooks. In 1992 the first in a series of five young readers' novels debuted with *The Glove of Darth Vader* by Paul and Hollace Davids. There then followed a fourteen-book series called *Young Jedi Knights* by Kevin Anderson and Rebecca Moesta, starring Jacen and Jaina, the teenage children of Han and Leia. A separate six-book series titled *Junior Jedi Knights* was also published in tandem and chronicled the adventures of Han and Leia's other child – eleven-year-old Anakin Solo.

With the release of the prequels, the focus of the young reader books shifted onto characters from those films, with the *Jedi Apprentice*, *Jedi Quest* and *Last of the Jedi* series, all by Jude Watson.

New young reader titles continue to be published and in more recent years these have been tied into the *Rebels* television show and the new films.

Cherished by young readers of a certain generation were the *Star Wars* storybooks. These were large format books telling the story of each of the films, accompanied by large

  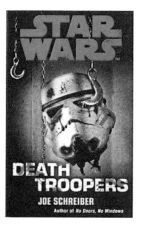 

   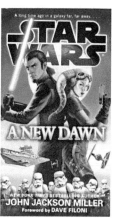

photographic illustrations. Each of the original films were released in both softcover and hardcover, and storybooks have continued to be issued for subsequent films.

The annual – a slim hardback book for children aimed at the Christmas market – has been a tradition in the UK for decades. The first *Star Wars* annual was released in 1978 and would become a yearly event with eight volumes published in total up until 1985, along with a further Ewoks annual in 1988. The annuals were mostly comprised of Marvel comic strip reprints. The first annual was released through Brown Watson, while the remainder of the '70s and '80s volumes were issued by Grandreams in association with Marvel. Annuals resumed in the nineties and continue to be issued yearly.

As well as fictional books there has also been an extensive library of *Star Wars* non-fiction titles. The earliest of these was the *Star Wars Sketch Book*, which was released by Ballantine in 1977, collecting many of the production sketches from the film. *The Art of Star Wars* followed shortly after, featuring production paintings and concept art. Follow-up volumes to both were released for each of the original trilogy films.

To tie in with the release of *The Empire Strikes Back*, *Once Upon a Galaxy: A Journal of the Making of The Empire Strikes Back* was released. This was a pocket-sized paperback written by Alan Arnold, and a similar title, *The Making of Return of the Jedi*, edited by John Philip Peecher, followed in 1983. More lavish 'Making Of' volumes followed for each of the prequel films and, to mark the 30th anniversary of the original movie, Del Rey released *The Making of Star Wars* – a large coffee table book comprehensively covering production of the film. Subsequent volumes followed to mark the 30th anniversaries of both *Empire* and *Jedi*.

Since the 1990s, the amount of *Star Wars* non-fiction titles has been enormous, with titles covering all aspects of the saga.

Due to the huge volumes printed, few *Star Wars* books are particularly valuable. However, decent condition copies of the earlier books are becoming hard to find.

While the vast library of *Star Wars* books can be a little daunting, there is no doubt that these books have played a huge part in expanding the saga, documenting its history and keeping the flame alive over the years.

The 1990s saw the launch of a dedicated young readers range.

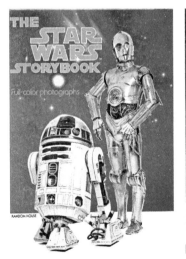

The Star Wars Storybooks are fondly remembered by older fans.

Early titles aimed at younger fans were simplistic picture books, such as *The Maverick Moon*.

Star Wars Annuals have been a tradition for many years.

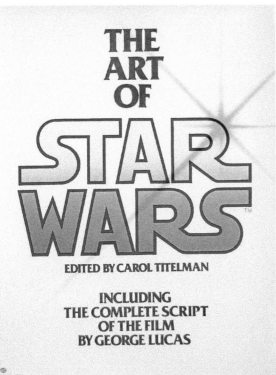

Above: *The Star Wars Sketch Book*.
(Ballantine, 1977)

Left: *The Art of Star Wars*.
(Ballantine, 1979)

Right: *Once Upon a Galaxy* was the first 'Making Of' book to be released for *Star Wars*.

Below: To celebrate the 30th anniversary this book detailed the production of the first movie in unprecedented depth.

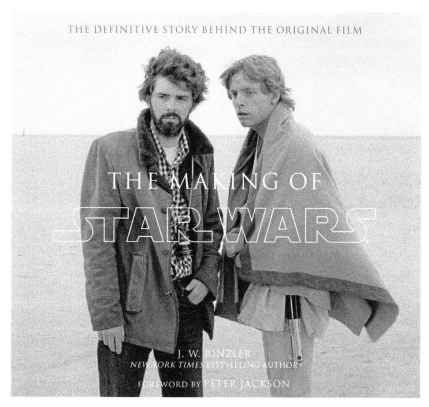

CHAPTER 5

Comics and Magazines

Star Wars was rooted in comic strip influences and Lucasfilm saw a *Star Wars* title as an essential tool in the marketing of the movie. A comic strip adaptation was to prove a hard sell, however, with both Warren and DC both declining approaches to publish *Star Wars*. Eventually, despite some reticence, Marvel Comics agreed to publish a six-part adaptation of the film.

Star Wars 1 was available just ahead of the movie, appearing on newsstands in April 1977. Roy Thomas took on writing duties with art by Howard Chaykin.

The comic was an instant hit, with sales of Issue 1 eventually surpassing a million copies, and the initial six-issue run was soon extended into an ongoing series of original stories.

Roy Thomas and Howard Chaykin departed the title fairly early on, with Archie Goodwin taking over writing duties for a period. David Micheline later wrote a large chunk of issues, while Jo Duffy penned much of the latter half of the run. On the art side, Carmine Infantino pencilled a large proportion of issues, with Walt Simonson, Ron Frenz, Tom Palmer and Cynthia Martin also enjoying lengthy runs.

The Empire Strikes Back was serialised in the comic over Issues 39–44, written by Archie Goodwin and with art by Al Williamson. Following the *Empire* adaptation, Goodwin and Williamson would enjoy a well-received run on a *Star Wars* newspaper strip.

Star Wars Issue 1. (Marvel, 1977)

The strip originated various memorable and recurring characters. These included Jaxxon (a green space bunny), Valance (a bounty hunter resembling the Terminator), the Tagge family, smuggling trio Rik Duel, Dani and Chihdo, Shira Brie (a spy for the Empire), Kiro (an aquatic alien) and Fenn Shysa (a Boba Fett-like Mandalorian).

After the films concluded with *Return of the Jedi,* the comic became the only official continuation of the *Star Wars* story. Luke's old nemesis Shira Brie turned up as a new Vader-like villain called Lumiya, and the galaxy was invaded by a race called the Nagai, who were in league with the Empire. After 107 issues, *Star Wars* wrapped up in June 1986 after a record nine-year run.

As well as the regular issues, Marvel also published three bumper-sized annual issues and serialised *Return of the Jedi* as a four-part miniseries. The movie adaptations were collected in various formats, including pocket-sized paperback compilations, oversized treasury editions and magazine-sized Marvel super specials. Marvel published short-lived comics based on the *Ewoks and Droids* animated series under their younger readers' Star Comics imprint and ran a separate *Star Wars* strip in *Pizzazz* magazine. There were also two paperback compilations: *Star Wars* and *Star Wars 2: World of Fire,* collecting the *Pizzazz* material along with strips previously only published in Britain.

In the UK, comics were, by tradition, published on a weekly rather than monthly schedule and *Star Wars* debuted from Marvel UK as a black and white title in February 1978. *Star Wars Weekly* reprinted the US strips with a regular US monthly being spread, on average, over two weekly issues. To bulk out the page count, various other sci-fi-themed strips such as *Star Lord* and the *Micronauts* were included. The title was

Above and overleaf. – US Marvel *Star Wars* comics.

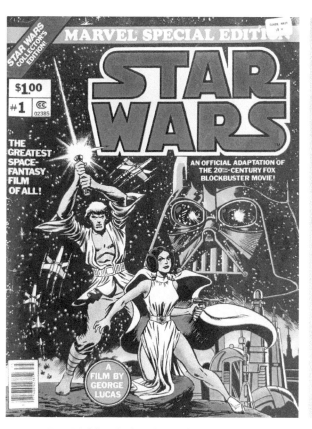

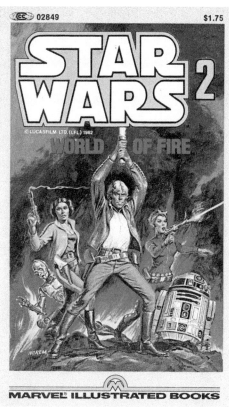

Above left: Marvel released several oversized *Star Wars* Treasury editions.

Above right: *World of Fire* was one of several paperback compilations released by Marvel.

renamed *Empire Strikes Back Weekly* in 1980, before switching to a monthly schedule later that year. In 1982 there was another name change to just *Star Wars* and the title concluded at Issue 171.

In 1983 Marvel relaunched *Star Wars* once again as a weekly entitled simply *Return of the Jedi*, with the numbering starting back at 1. The comic ran to 155 issues, ceasing publication in June 1986. The *Star Wars* strip then continued for a couple more months in Marvel UK's *Spider-Man and Zoids* title. Marvel UK also published various summer and winter specials, and there was also a short-lived *Ewoks* comic along with two *Droids* specials.

The US Marvel comics are now highly collectable, with both the first and last issues being particularly desirable. The UK comics are generally less sought after and can still be picked up relatively cheaply, although the first two issues command high prices if they come with the free cardboard X-Wing and TIE Fighter gifts.

In 1987, Blackthorne briefly inherited the license and published a three-issue run of *Star Wars* 3D comics. The comic was released quarterly and each issue came with a pair of 3D specs.

Marvel briefly considered a return to *Star Wars* comics in the late eighties and planned to publish a miniseries from Tom Veitch and Cam Kennedy under their more mature Epic Comics imprint.

Above and opposite above: British Marvel *Star Wars* comics.

Above: Despite plans for at least six issues, only three comics were released in Blackthorne's *Star Wars 3D* line.

Right: *Dark Empire* marked a new era for *Star Wars* comics as Dark Horse took over the license.

Dark Horse *Star Wars* comics.

Ultimately, the miniseries would find a home at Dark Horse comics. Dark Horse was a small press label that were having some success with licensed titles. The six-issue miniseries titled *Dark Empire* was published in 1991 and continued the story five years after *Return of the Jedi,* with Emperor Palpatine returning in a new cloned body. The comics were a hit and soon Dark Horse were publishing further *Star Wars* titles. They next turned to the Goodwin/Williamson *Star Wars* newspaper strips. With some reformatting and colouring, these formed the basis of *Classic Star Wars*, which enjoyed a twenty-issue run, followed by a second run of nine issues titled *Classic Star Wars: The Early Adventures*, collecting the earlier Russ Manning newspaper strips. While *Star Wars* spin-off fiction had to this point centred around the era of the original trilogy and the few years immediately after, Dark Horse took a creative leap with its next title. *Tales of the Jedi* told of events 4,000 years before *A New Hope*. Seven miniseries were released in total, with some journeying even further back into the timeline.

As the interest in *Star Wars* grew during the mid-nineties, Dark Horse began to pump out an increasing number of titles, primarily in the miniseries format. Two sequels to *Dark Empire* followed, there were also adaptations of some of the books including *Splinter of the Mind's Eye* and Timothy Zahn's Thrawn Trilogy. Dark Horse issued a six-part miniseries for 1996 crossmedia event *Shadows of the Empire,* and to coincide with the 1997 *Star Wars* Special Editions an all new adaptation of *A New Hope* was released. The dawn of a new trilogy with the release of *Star Wars: Episode 1* led to adaptations of each of the prequel films.

Although Dark Horse had initially favoured the miniseries format, they gradually began to delve into longer ongoing titles. *X-Wing Rogue Squadron* ran for thirty-five

Dark Horse comic adaptations of the films.

issues and was written by Michael A Stackpole who also penned a series of X-Wing novels, while *Star Wars Tales* – an anthology title featuring a wide range of stories from various well-known comic creators – clocked up twenty-four issues.

The first comic since the eighties to be just called *Star Wars* launched in 1998 and initially featured Ki Adi Mundi from the upcoming *Episode 1* as the lead protagonist. The comic gradually began to tie in closer to the events of the movies, with characters such as Anakin and Obi Wan featuring in storylines. With Issue 49 the comic became *Star Wars Republic*. The title is notable for originating the character of Aayla Secura, who went on to feature in both *Attack of the Clones* and *Revenge of the Sith*. Following the demise of *Republic* with Issue 83, Dark Horse launched another title, *Dark Times*, which was set following the events of *Revenge of the Sith*. *Dark Times* ran for seventeen regular issues followed by three miniseries.

While the ongoing *Star Wars* title told stories set in the prequel era, Dark Horse launched a second ongoing title, *Star Wars Empire*, which was set in the period of the original trilogy. This ran for forty issues before being replaced by a similar title – *Star Wars Rebellion,* which enjoyed a sixteen-issue run.

Other ongoing titles of the mid-2000s were more adventurous in their settings. *Knights of the Old Republic* journeyed back nearly 4,000 years, with stories set some years after the events of *Tales of the Jedi*. Another title would delve into the far future of the *Star Wars* saga; *Star Wars Legacy* was set 137 years after the events of *A New Hope* and followed the exploits of Cade Skywalker, a descendant of Luke. The title ran for fifty regular issues and a six-issue miniseries before being revived for a second eighteen-issue run, this time following the adventures of Han Solo's great, great, granddaughter, Ania Solo.

The second run of *Legacy* was one of several titles curtailed due to the expiration of Dark Horse's *Star Wars* license at the end of 2014. The latter years of Dark Horse's *Star Wars* line saw a fresh burst of creativity. *Agent of the Empire* was *Star Wars'* answer to 007, starring Imperial agent Jahan Cross, while *Dawn of the Jedi* chronicled the formation of the Jedi over 36,000 years before *A New Hope*. Another ongoing title once again called just *Star Wars* told stories in the aftermath of *A New Hope* and ran for twenty issues. In 2013 one of the most landmark *Star Wars* comics ever was released. *The Star Wars* was an eight-part adaptation of an early George Lucas *Star Wars* draft from 1974, which was markedly different to the eventual film.

Over the twenty-three years of their license, Dark Horse published over 800 individual *Star Wars* comics. Many issues also had variant covers and there have been numerous

Dark Horse *Star Wars* comics.

compilations in the popular graphic novel format. Due to Disney's restructuring of the *Star Wars* Expanded Universe, a majority of Dark Horse's *Star Wars* output is now no longer considered part of the official canon, and while there aren't many issues that currently fetch premium prices, this could well change in the future.

In 2015, Marvel, now also part of Disney, returned to the *Star Wars* galaxy, spearheading their range with a comic once again simply dubbed *Star Wars*. Other titles soon followed featuring characters such as Darth Vader, Kanan and Poe Dameron. Alongside their various regular titles, Marvel have also released various miniseries, along with adaptations of the new movies. Most of the new Marvel *Star Wars* comics have been released in numerous cover variants with varying levels of rarity. In a little over three years, Marvel have now published more *Star Wars* comics than they did during their original nine-year run.

As well as continuing the saga's adventures in strip form, there have also been various publications over the years that have documented the films. One of the earliest was the *Star Wars Album*, sold in the UK as *The Star Wars Collector's Edition*. The magazine doubled as a promotional tool for the movie and featured many spreads from classic Hollywood films as the makers attempted to place *Star Wars* in context for the film going public. Further collectors' magazines have since followed for all the live action films to date.

Marvel resumed publication on *Star Wars* comics in 2015.

Star Wars Collector's Edition magazines.

Star Wars poster magazines.

Another early title was the *Star Wars Poster Magazine*, which was first released in 1977. Eighteen issues were published in total. Further poster magazines followed for *The Empire Strikes Back*, *Return of the Jedi*, the *Star Wars* Special Editions and *Episode 1*.

An actual ongoing *Star Wars* magazine would not be realised for many years; however, members of the *Star Wars* Fan Club would receive a newsletter simply headed 'The Official *Star Wars* Fan Club' for the first few issues but was retitled 'Bantha Tracks' from Issue 5. In 1987 the *Star Wars* Fan Club was rebranded the Lucasfilm Fan Club and a more lavish publication was launched, which also covered the company's other properties. As *Star Wars* became popular again in the nineties, the magazine was retitled *Star Wars Insider* from Issue 23 and continues to be published to this day.

In the UK, a parallel publication was launched by Titan in 1996, entitled *Star Wars Magazine*. The magazine included original articles as well as Dark Horse comic strip reprints in its early issues. As the title continued, it began to have less UK-originated content and would reprint material from the *Star Wars Insider*, before eventually becoming just a UK version of the *Insider*.

In the nineties another ongoing publication was *Star Wars Galaxy Magazine*. The magazine, published by Topps, came polybagged with a free poster and *Star Wars* trading cards. Thirteen quarterly issues were released in total before the magazine was relaunched as *Star Wars Galaxy Collector* in 1998, which lasted only eight issues.

The *Star Wars* Fan Club newsletter eventually evolved into the *Star Wars Insider Magazine*, which continues to be published to this day.

Starlog Magazine, which had regularly featured *Star Wars* articles, also produced three issues of the *Star Wars Technical Journal* in 1994.

With the growth in digital downloads of both comics and magazines, the printed word continues to be under threat. Nevertheless, the popularity of *Star Wars* and the strength of its collectors' base mean *Star Wars* publications will likely be with us for a long time to come.

Above left: *Star Wars Magazine* Issue 1. (Titan, 1996)

Above right: *Star Wars Galaxy Magazine* Issue 1. (Topps, 1994)

Below: *Star Wars Technical Journal* magazines. (Starlog, 1994)

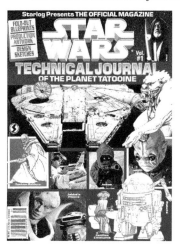

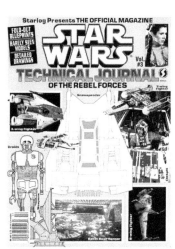

CHAPTER 6

Trading Cards and Stickers

America has a long history of collectable cards, with the first baseball cards dating back to the nineteenth century. In the 1950s bubble gum cards became popular, and by the 1970s Topps were publishing cards on a variety of properties including *Planet of the Apes* and *Star Trek*. Topps debuted their first *Star Wars* cards in 1977 and have gone on to enjoy a long relationship with the saga.

The initial set comprised sixty-six cards and eleven sticker cards. The cards came in packets containing ten cards, one sticker card and a strip of gum. The backs of the cards featured a mixture of information and sections of a picture puzzle. The initial set featured a blue border on the cards. Further sets quickly followed, with each set having different coloured borders, making them easy to differentiate. A second and third series were also released in 1977 featuring red and yellow borders, with numbering continuing on from the first set. Series 4 and 5 followed in 1978 with green and orange borders.

Series 3 threw up an interesting variant of card 207. Initial editions appeared to show C-3PO sporting a rather phallic looking appendage. Topps withdrew the card and reissued it with an airbrushed version. Although the revised card was actually produced in lower numbers, the notoriety of the original ensures it is the more collectable of the two.

The sets for *The Empire Strikes Back* were nearly double the length of those for the previous film and three series were released in total. Alphabet letter stickers were also introduced. Due to *Return of the Jedi*'s shorter shelf life, only two sets were released. The Series 1 Jedi stickers are unusual in that different colour border variants were produced.

In 1978 Topps produced *Star Wars* Sugar-Free Gum, apparently in response to a request from George Lucas, who suffered from diabetes. Although no cards were issued in the packs, the wrappers opened up into mini pin-ups, with fifty-six different images being available. There was also a set of thirty giant photo cards for *The Empire Strikes Back,* with one card being released in each pack.

In the UK Topps cards were distributed by Trebor, but British fans didn't get the full product run, with only the blue and red *Star Wars* sets and the first *Empire* set being released. All the sets omitted the sticker cards and the red *Star Wars* set featured a different order and numbering to the US release. *The Empire Strikes Back* alphabet sticker cards were also issued as a separate release, entitled Initials stickers.

While original *Star Wars* Topps cards are collectable, it is reasonably easy to find sets in near mint condition due to the large amount of unopened boxes that have survived over the years. Prices are still affordable enough for collectors to purchase complete sets, and outside of the withdrawn C-3PO, there is little value for single cards. Top prices go to unopened retail boxes, known as wax boxes.

A selection of original Topps wrappers.

Star Wars Sugar-Free Gum wrappers. (Topps, 1979)

In 1993 Topps returned to *Star Wars* after a decade-long break. In the intervening years, the collectable card market had undergone a change, with bubble gum cards making way for glossy collectable cards that were sold primarily through specialist stores. Regular releases resumed with *Star Wars* Galaxy – a set showcasing the art of the saga. The success of the cards led to further *Star Wars* Galaxy releases, with seven series having been issued to date.

Topps returned to the roots of the saga, with sets based around each of the original movies but rendered in a longer widescreen format. Widevision sets were issued for each of the prequel movies, and *Episode 2* and *Episode 3* also received standard-sized cards.

Above and below: Original Topps cards from the 1970s and 1980s.

The Empire Strikes Back giant photo cards. (Topps, 1980)

Other notable releases over the years include *Shadows of the Empire* (an all-art set based on the 1996 multimedia event), *Star Wars* 3Di (widevision cards featuring lenticular images from the films), various series that returned to the classic stock and look of the original bubble gum cards, sets based on both *Clone Wars* animated projects and celebratory releases for both the 30th and 40th anniversaries.

A popular feature of Topps *Star Wars* sets from the 1990s onwards are the chase cards. These are cards usually printed on special stock, making up a smaller subset and inserted into packs at a lower ratio than regular cards.

In the 2000s, Topps began introducing autographed cards into boxes. The majority of the main cast members from the movies have now signed with Topps, as well as various supporting players and behind-the-scenes personnel. Odds on the autograph cards vary widely, with the amount of cards signed by leading actors being far fewer than those autographed by supporting artists. This makes full sets of many of the releases almost impossible to compile. Some autographed cards such as those from Harrison Ford have often only been available in single figures and have sold for four figure sums whenever they have appeared in online auctions.

Artist sketch cards have also proved a popular addition to many releases. Cards feature hand-drawn sketches, and cards from certain artists tend to be more prolific than others. Recently, artefact cards have appeared in some sets, which feature actual pieces of costumes and props that were used in the movies.

The recent slate of new films has seen Topps continue their relationship with the saga with sets for *The Force Awakens*, *Rogue One* and *The Last Jedi*.

As one of the longest serving *Star Wars* licenses, there is no doubt that Topps and *Star Wars* will be a partnership that will continue for many years to come.

A selection of Topps modern *Star Wars* cards.

Various autographed Topps *Star Wars* trading cards.

Various Decipher CCG cards.

As well as the standard type of trading card designed to be collected and traded, there have also been trading cards that operate as components in a game. Decipher released the *Star Wars* Customisable Card Game in 1995 with the first set simply titled Premiere. The set consisted of 324 cards, all from the original movie. Cards were released in packs in three rarity levels: rare, uncommon and common. A rare card would only appear once in a pack, while there would be several uncommons and commons. Cards were split into several categories including characters, ships, creatures, locations, devices and weapons. There were also cards with specific functions, known as interrupts and effects. Players had to pick a side in gameplay and could choose whether to play a light side or dark side deck.

Further releases followed, including *A New Hope,* featuring more material from the first movie, and then sets themed around specific environments, including Hoth, Dagobah and Cloud City for *The Empire Strikes Back* and Jabbas Palace, Endor and Death Star 2 for *Return of the Jedi*. A Special Edition set was also released featuring material that supplemented previous sets. The final three *Star Wars* CCG sets – Tatooine, Coruscant and Theed Palace – introduced *Episode 1* content to the game.

Later Decipher releases incorporated chase foil variants and alternate-image versions of certain cards.

The Empire Strikes Back sticker album. (FKS, 1980)

As well as the regular expansion sets, Decipher also put out a number of boxed and special releases. Several sets came with accompanying starter decks. There were also two-player games, boxed anthology sets, enhanced versions of several releases and a series called Reflections, which revisited previous cards on shiny foil-coated stock. Unlimited editions were made available of the first four expansions, which can be identified by a white border on the cards rather than the black on the regular limited versions.

As well as the main CCG, Decipher also issued two separate spin-off games. To accompany the launch of *Star Wars: Episode 1,* there was a game titled Young Jedi, which was aimed at a younger audience. Five expansions, two enhanced editions and

Return of the Jedi sticker album. (Panini, 1983)

a reflections series were released in total. There was also a brief attempt at a third game using computer-generated imagery titled Jedi Knights, but only three sets were released.

Decipher's *Star Wars* license came to an end in 2001 due to the purchase of Decipher's rival, Wizards of the Coast, by Hasbro. To tie in with *Episode 2: Attack of the Clones*, Wizards introduced their own CCG, entitled the *Star Wars* Trading Card Game, but this was totally incompatible with the Decipher cards and was to alienate much of the player base. Ten sets were issued with the final release coinciding with *Revenge of the Sith*.

In the UK, a popular children's pastime is sticker collecting. One of the chief sticker manufacturers is Italian company Panini, who produced stickers and an album for the first film, although these were never issued in the UK, just Italy and Germany.

UK collectors had to wait until *The Empire Strikes Back* for their *Star Wars* sticker fix, with FKS issuing stickers and an accompanying album. Panini then returned to *Star Wars* with UK stickers and an album for *Return of the Jedi*, which were also issued in the US by Topps. There was then a considerable gap before Panini's next release, which coincided with the 1997 Special Editions. For the prequels, the license passed to Merlin, a subsidiary of Topps, and *Star Wars* sticker albums continue to be released on a regular basis.

The early stickers and albums are now collectable, particularly if the album is unfilled and the stickers are unapplied.

While stickers and cards may seem quaint in today's digital world, with Topps now offering *Star Wars* digital cards and trading apps, the *Star Wars* collector will always prefer something more tangible. Just as baseball cards are still being enjoyed over a hundred years after their first appearance, who's to say *Star Wars* fans won't be trading cards and pasting stickers well into the future.

CHAPTER 7

Home Entertainment

Today it is easy to take for granted the fact that you can watch a *Star Wars* film at your own convenience. However, it wasn't always so easy. In the late '70s and early '80s, you could look out for the film in a rerun at cinemas, but other options were strictly limited.

While the whole film remained exclusively in the domain of theatres, fans at least had a chance of owning parts of it. An early commercial release of *Star Wars* footage came in Kenner's *Star Wars* Movie Viewer – a plastic hand-cranked camera that came with a cartridge containing clips from the film. Four further cassettes featuring longer sequences were released separately. The *Star Wars* viewer and cartridges were modelled on an existing design Kenner had been using for some years.

While the Kenner viewer was marketed as a children's toy, the more seasoned film enthusiast had another option to view *Star Wars* footage at home. Super 8 mm film was a popular format for making home movies, but there was also a niche market for commercially releasing footage from feature films.

Ken Films released *Star Wars* 8 mm footage in a number of forms. There was a short eight-minute reel, available in both colour/sound and as cheaper colour/silent and black and white/silent options. Two longer reels were also issued in colour/sound format only, running to around seventeen minutes. There were also widescreen Cineascope and Cineavison versions of one of the longer compilations.

Ken Films repeated the formula for *The Empire Strikes Back*, once again with one short and two longer compilations, all available as colour/sound options only.

Kenner's Movie Viewer was also marketed for other properties, including *The Six Million Dollar Man* and *Alien*.

Star Wars Super 8 mm reels from Ken Films.

The short version actually came with a cassette containing the soundtrack for those with projectors that didn't have sound capabilities.

The Super 8 mm films are interesting for a number of quirks on several releases, including a voice over in place of the opening crawl, and actor and production credits at the front of the movie. By the early eighties the growth of home video had all but killed the demand for Super 8 mm and there were no Ken Films releases for *Return of the Jedi*.

The story of *Star Wars* on Super 8 mm didn't end there, however. In 1989, Derann film services released the entire original movie. The film was released over four 600 ft spools with the cover boxes strangely featuring part of the poster art from *Return of the Jedi*. Mono and stereo versions were available. Derann followed this with a four-reel set for *Return of the Jedi*.

The arrival of home video technology provided a more viable way to market films for domestic viewing. The initial high retail cost of video tapes meant films were usually rented and video shops became a common sight in the 1980s. In these early years there were two main competing formats, VHS and Betamax, and most movies would be released on both.

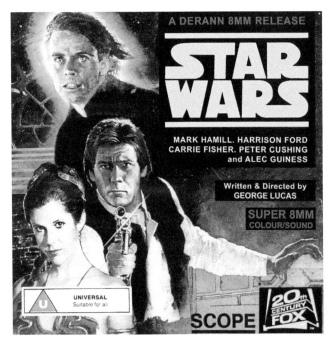

Derann released the complete first movie on Super 8 mm in 1989.

UK *Star Wars* rental video tapes.

The first *Star Wars* home video release was actually a television special on the making of the first movie released by Magnetic Video in 1979. In those days there was more mileage to be gained from withholding big tent-pole films from video release as they could be re-released theatrically. *Star Wars* finally appeared in 1982 from 20th Century Fox Video, with *The Empire Strikes Back* having a similarly belated release in 1984 from CBS/Fox Video, along with a separate 'Making of' documentary *SPFX: The Empire Strikes Back*. While by 1986 *Star Wars* had all but been put in mothballs, one last spark of life came with the long-awaited video release of *Return of the Jedi*.

In America, two Ewok movies had been produced for television broadcast, but these were reserved for a limited theatrical run and for home video release across Europe. *Caravan of Courage* was released by CBS/Fox in 1985, while *Battle of Endor* was issued by MGM/UA Video in 1988 on VHS only.

Although the *Star Wars* rental tapes could be bought through specialist dealers, the retail price was high, at around £70 a tape. Most of the cassettes that are in circulation today are from when stores sold them off after they had outlived their shelf life. The *Star Wars* and *Empire* tapes were released prior to the implementation of the 1984 Video Recordings Act and can be easily identified from later sell-through versions as they are uncertified.

By the mid-eighties, VHS had eclipsed Betamax as the preferred format, and prices had dropped enough for tapes to be sold on the high street direct to the consumer. *Star Wars* first arrived on the sell-through market in 1987, priced at around £10. It was then re-released the following year alongside the first sell-through releases of *Empire* and *Jedi*. The films would regularly be rereleased on video throughout the eighties and nineties with different sleeve designs and new attractions such as widescreen letterboxing and remastering to try and persuade fans to rebuy the films. In 1995 Fox issued the limited edition '*Star Wars* Trilogy: Definitive Collectors Edition' set, which came in a metal tin titled 'ISD Executor'. As well as containing all three original movies, the set also included various documentaries, complete scripts to all three films

A store display promoting the release of
The Empire Strikes Back on video.

and a selection of prints. By the 2000s video was slowly being usurped by the rival format of DVD and *Revenge of the Sith* was to mark the final *Star Wars* video release.

As well as the films, there were also sell-through releases of *Battle of Endor*, *Droids and Ewoks* animated series episodes and several of the documentaries.

The emergence of DVD as the dominant home entertainment format resulted in a massive purge, with many tapes being thrown away. Today there is a slow dawning that video may have some nostalgia appeal after all. Rental copies of the first movie from 1982 are hard to find as the title had a relatively short shelf life since it was shown on ITV the same year. *Revenge of the Sith* is also rare on VHS since it was produced in low numbers due to the declining market for video.

Another less prolific format for home entertainment from the eighties and nineties was laserdisc. This involved a large LP-sized disc, which had to be turned half-way through. The format never really broke through into the mainstream but was popular with film enthusiasts. In the UK, laserdisc versions of all three original trilogy films were issued in tandem with their original video releases. *Empire* and *Jedi* were issued in partnership with SG Records & Video. 20th Century Fox also collaborated with the UK company Encore Entertainment on a boxset of the Special Editions in 1997.

In the US the original trilogy was reissued on laserdisc several times throughout the eighties and nineties and these often made their way to the UK collectors' market.

Various *Star Wars* video releases.

A milestone release was the '*Star Wars* Trilogy: The Definitive Collection' set. This contained nine discs incorporating various bonus features and commentaries and also included a hardcover book – *George Lucas: The Creative Impulse*. Laserdisc had all but fizzled out by the time of the prequels, although the format was still popular enough in Japan for *The Phantom Menace* to be released there.

Star Wars first arrived on DVD with the 2001 release of *Episode 1* and the *Clone Wars* movie marked the debut of *Star Wars* on Blu-ray in 2009. Most of the DVDs and Blu-rays are still available; however, several of the early DVDs have been deleted and are becoming sought after. These include 2006 releases of the original trilogy, which came with a second disc carrying unrestored versions of the original cuts, a compilation of the two Ewoks films, the 2003–05 *Clone Wars* micro series and selection of *Droids and Ewoks* animated episodes.

The release of Star Wars on sell through was promoted with this store display.

MAY THE VIDEO BE WITH YOU!

The '*Star Wars* Trilogy:
Definitive Collection'
set. (20th Century Fox
Video, 1995)

Star Wars laserdiscs.

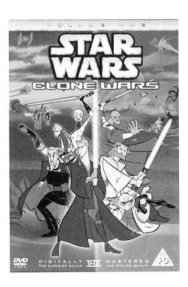

Several of the *Star Wars* DVDs from the 2000s have now been deleted.

Star Wars soundtrack LP. (20th Century Fox Records, 1977)

Another way of experiencing the saga in the early days was through sound, with various releases on record and cassette. 20th Century Fox released the official soundtracks for all three films. The LP for the first movie was by far the most prestigious, with two 12 inch discs in a gatefold sleeve and a free poster.

In the days before home video, the nearest many could get to experiencing the events of the film was the 'Story of *Star Wars*' – an abridged version of the film's audio with narration. Similar volumes were released for both *Empire* and *Jedi*.

An interesting curiosity was the audio play *Rebel Mission to Ord Mantell*, written by Brian Daley. Although none of the original actors reprised their parts, the play is notable for being the first attempt at an original *Star Wars* story in this medium.

An earlier attempt at *Star Wars* in audio form had been the radio plays also written by Daley. An adaptation of the first movie was broadcast on National Public Radio in the US in 1981 and on Radio 1 in the UK. The play, broadcast in thirteen episodes, followed the story of the film, but with many new and expanded scenes. Mark Hamill and Anthony Daniels reprised their respective roles, with Billy Dee Williams joining them for a ten-part adaptation of *Empire* in 1983.

The radio plays were never commercially released until 1993, when Highbridge Audio issued both serials on CD and cassette. They proved popular enough for Highbridge to fund production of a six-part *Return of the Jedi* adaptation. Anthony Daniels was the only original cast member to return for the 1996 *Jedi* production.

CD quickly supplanted cassette and vinyl sales from the nineties and there have been many *Star Wars* soundtrack releases in the format over the last few decades. More recently, vinyl has made a comeback, leading to reissues of old material in the format as well as new releases.

Another way to bring *Star Wars* home was through the video games. Consoles and home computers surged in popularity during the 1980s and Parker Brothers were the first to issue *Star Wars* games. *The Empire Strikes Back* was the debut release in 1982. This was a scrolling shooter game involving Luke's Snowspeeder facing off against AT-ATs. The game was initially released for the Atari 2600 and later the Mattel

The Story of Star Wars record.
(Superscope, 1977)

Intelvision. 1983 saw the release of several *Star Wars* games including *Return of the Jedi: Death Star Battle* for various Atari systems and the ZX Spectrum. The game involved you piloting the *Millennium Falcon*, shooting up TIE Fighters and attempting to destroy the Death Star. *Jedi Arena* for the Atari 2600 was based around the scene from the first movie where Luke uses the Jedi training ball. There was also a home release for the *Star Wars Arcade* game, which was issued on various systems. Arcade versions of *Empire* and *Jedi*, along with a reissue of *Star Wars*, were made available by Domark in the late 1980s.

As *Star Wars* began to take off in popularity again in the 1990s, *Star Wars* games began to be issued frequently with increasing levels of sophistication. Most games from the 1990s on were released through Lucasfilm's own video game division: Lucasarts.

From their humble beginnings as simplistic shooting games, the *Star Wars* games have grown to include immersive worlds. They also came to be recognised as part of the official canon, and characters originating from the games, such as Darth Revan and Darth Malgus, have become as iconic as many of those from the movies.

Today there are more ways than ever to enjoy *Star Wars* at home, and it is easy to forget those long past days when the only way to get the full experience was in a cinema.

1990s compact disc releases of the Star Wars radio plays from Highbridge Audio.

Rebel Mission to Ord Mantell record. (Buena Vista Records, 1983)

Late 1980s home versions of the *Star Wars* arcade games.

The Empire Strikes Back video game. (Parker Bros, 1982)

A promotional poster for Parker Bros' *Jedi Arena* game.